BOOKWORKS

CREATIVE LITERATURE ACTIVITIES
FOR USE IN WHOLE-LANGUAGE PROGRAMS

- PLOT - SETTING
- CHARACTERIZATION

GRADES 4-8

WRITTEN BY PAMELA AMICK KLAWITTER, ED.D.
ILLUSTRATED BY CAROL KRIEGER

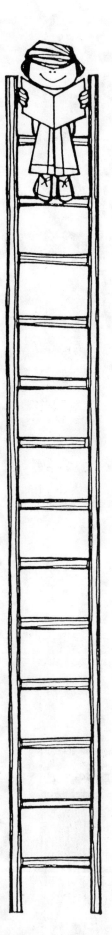

The Learning Works

Cover design by Beverly Armstrong

Copyright ©1993
The Learning Works, Inc.
Santa Barbara, California 93160
Printed in the United States of America

Contents

Introduction

Bookworks is a literature-based reading program designed to develop writing and critical thinking skills and to promote a life-long love of reading. **Bookworks** helps to increase a student's understanding of the role characterization, plot, setting, and vocabulary play in the composition of a good book. The activities in this book help students learn to identify and evaluate the components of literature and to transfer those concepts to their own writing.

Bookworks is designed for students in grades 4–8. It includes activities that can be used as part of a whole literature approach to teaching reading, as a supplement to a basal reading program, or as an independent reading program.

A Student Record Page is included to help keep track of the number and types of activities each student has completed. Also included is a reading list of classic literature for children that features Newbery Award winners and Honor books from 1922 to the present. Another list features classics and time-honored favorites in children's literature. These lists are ideal to send home at holiday time or for summer vacation to guide parents in selecting appropriate books for their children.

Name _____

Character Reference

> The **characters** are the people, animals, or imaginary creatures that participate in the action of the story. In most stories, the **main character** is the center of the action. Less important characters in the story are called **minor characters**.

Complete the sentences below by describing events found in your book.

Title _____

Author _____

Main Character _____

1. The main character did a funny thing when_____

   _____

   _____

2. The smartest thing the main character did was _____

   _____

   _____

3. The main character reacted exactly as I would have when _____

   _____

   _____

4. A really unbelievable thing the main character did was_____

   _____

   _____

5. Draw a portrait of the main character on the back of your paper.

Name _____

Personality Profile

Authors use different ways to describe a character's personality. Find eight passages in the book you read that helped you understand the main character's personality. Write the page number and passage that describes the character in the spaces below.

Examples from *Caddie Woodlawn* by Carol Ryrie Brink:

page 1   "…Caddie Woodlawn was eleven, and as wild a tomboy as ever ran the woods of western Wisconsin."

page 15   "I want you to let Caddie run wild with the boys. Don't keep her in the house learning to be a lady."

Title _____

Author _____

Main Character _____

Page _____ 1. _____

_____

_____

Page _____ 2. _____

_____

_____

Page _____ 3. _____

_____

Name _____

Personality Profile
(continued)

Page _____ 4. _____

_____

_____

Page _____ 5. _____

_____

_____

Page _____ 6. _____

_____

_____

Page _____ 7. _____

_____

_____

Page _____ 8. _____

_____

_____

Challenge: On a separate sheet of paper, describe your main character in a two-paragraph sketch.

Name _____

Who Am I?

Most characters can be identified in a variety of ways. In *Ramona the Pest* by Beverly Cleary, Ramona might be called Beezus's sister, Henry's pesky neighbor, Miss Binney's student, a six-year-old, etc. Choose three characters from your book and describe them in as many ways as possible.

Title _____

Author _____

Character 1_____
　　　　　　　　　name

_____

_____

_____

_____

_____

_____

_____

_____

_____

_____

Name _____

Who Am I?
(continued)

Character 2 _____
                        name

_____

_____

_____

_____

_____

_____

_____

_____

Character 3 _____
                        name

_____

_____

_____

_____

_____

_____

_____

_____

_____

_____

_____

Name _____

Character Comparison

In what ways are you similar to the main character in your book? How are you different? Fill in the chart below comparing yourself to the main character. On a separate sheet of paper, write a short essay describing ways you are alike and different using your chart to help you organize your thoughts.

Title _____

Author _____

Your Name _____	Character's Name _____
_____	_____
_____	_____
_____	_____
_____	_____
_____	_____
_____	_____
_____	_____
_____	_____

Name _____

Letter Perfect

Pretend you are a character from your book. Write a letter to another character in the same book. In your letter, discuss people and events from the story.

Title _____

Author _____

Dear _____ ,

_____

_____

_____

_____

_____

_____

_____

_____

_____

_____

_____

_____

_____

_____

Sincerely,

_____

Name _____

That's Life

Complete each sentence using characters and events from your book.

Title _____

Author _____

1. _____ cooperated with _____

   when _____

   _____.

2. _____ showed the real meaning of friendship

   when _____

   _____.

3. _____ had to make an important choice when

   _____

   _____.

Name _____

That's Life

(continued)

4. The hardest thing _____ had to do was

   _____

   _____ .

5. _____ really cared about _____

   _____

   _____ .

6. _____ was happiest when _____

   _____

   _____ .

7. A good example of sharing occurred when _____

   _____

   _____ .

Name _____

Changing Times

Choose a character from your book. In the boxes below, draw this character as he/she might have looked at three different times in the story. Tell what is happening in each picture you draw.

Title _____

Author _____

Character _____

1. _____

   _____

   _____

   _____

   _____

   _____

2. _____

   _____

   _____

   _____

   _____

   _____

3. _____

   _____

   _____

   _____

   _____

   _____

Name _____

Casting Director

Sometimes characters in the books we read remind us of people we know. Imagine that you have been asked to cast a movie based on your book. Select two characters from the book, and choose people you actually know to play each part. Make your choice based on similarities between the character's and the actor's physical appearance or personality. Then write a summary of your movie focusing on the roles these two characters play.

Title _____

Author _____

Character 1 _____

I chose _____ to play this role

because _____

_____

_____

_____

Character 2 _____

I chose _____ to play this role

because _____

_____

_____

Name _____

Sharp Contrast

Choose two characters from your book. Write one name at the top of each column below. List personal characteristics in each column that show how the two differ from one another.

Example: *Little Red Riding Hood*

<u>Little Red</u>	<u>Wolf</u>
human	animal
two legs	four legs
thoughtful of others	mean and cruel

Title _____

Author _____

Name _____   Name_____

_____   _____

_____   _____

_____   _____

_____   _____

_____   _____

_____   _____

_____   _____

_____   _____

_____   _____

_____   _____

Name _____

Feelings

Find three passages that help you understand how the main character is feeling at three different points in the story. Write the page reference, the passage, and one sentence telling why the character felt the way he/she did.

Example: *Stone Fox* by John Reynolds Gardiner
Main Character: Little Willy

page 15   (passage from book) "His eyes were wild with excitement."

(explanation) Little Willy had begun to work out a hand signal code with Grandfather, who hadn't spoken in over three weeks.

Title _____

Author _____

Main Character _____

Page _____ (passage) _____

(explanation) _____

_____

_____

Page _____ (passage) _____

(explanation) _____

_____

_____

Page _____ (passage) _____

(explanation) _____

_____

_____

Name _____

Character Web

Making a character web is a way to get a complete picture of the character's personality. Use the web on the following page to organize ideas about the main character in your book.

1. Write the character's name in the center of the web.

2. Jot down as many thoughts as you can relating to the topic listed inside each circle.

3. Once all of your ideas are written down, write a five-paragraph character sketch. Build a paragraph around the ideas from each different circle on the web.

Topics

relationships	Who are the character's friends and family?
appearance	What does the character look like?
others' opinions	What do others think of the main character?
personality	What is the character like as a person?
hobbies/interests	What does the character enjoy doing in his/her spare time?

Title _____

Author _____

Name _____

Character Web
(continued)

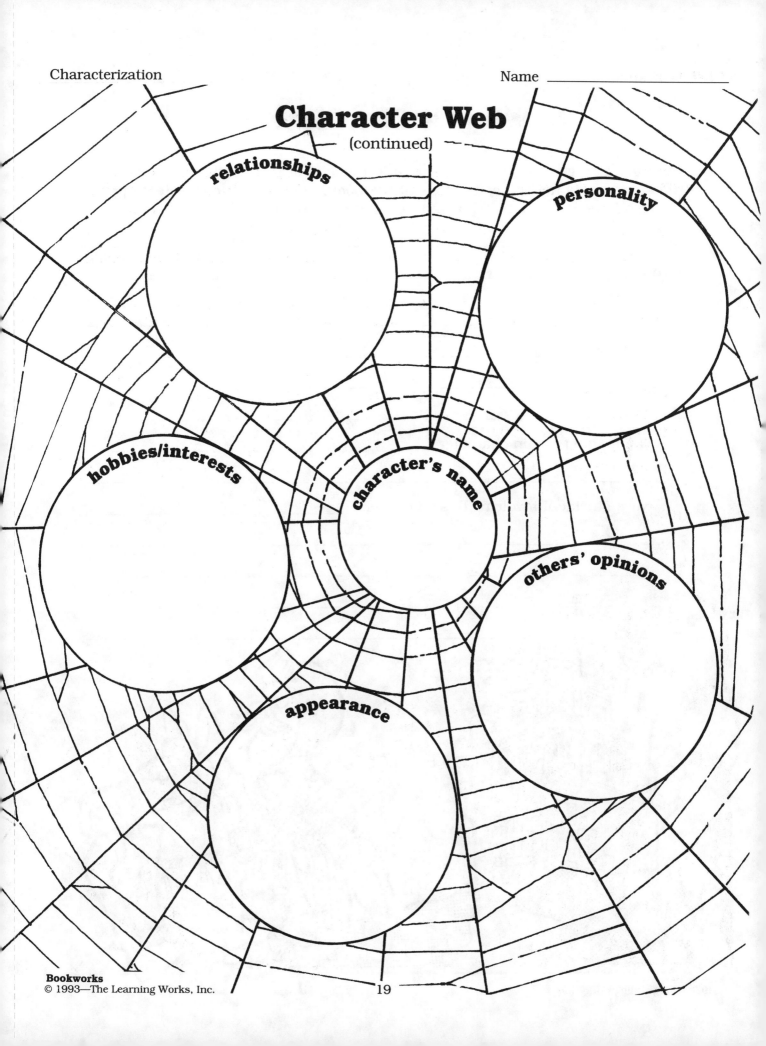

relationships

personality

hobbies/interests

character's name

others' opinions

appearance

Name _____

What a Character!

A **minor character** is a person or animal that interacts with the main character in a story but is not the main focus of the book. Some minor characters appear briefly; others quite often. Tell about two minor characters from your book.

Title _____

Author _____

1. Name _____

   Description _____

   _____

   _____

   Relationship to main character _____

   _____

   Favorite incident involving this character _____

   _____

   _____

   _____

   _____

Name _____

What a Character!
(continued)

2. Name _____

   Description _____

   _____

   _____

   Relationship to main character _____

   _____

   Favorite incident involving this character _____

   _____

   _____

   _____

   _____

On a separate piece of white art paper, draw pictures of the two characters you selected using things you learned about their physical appearance in your book.

Name _____

Diamonte

A **diamonte** is a poem written in the shape of a diamond that contrasts two subjects and makes a comparison between them by moving from one to the other.

Diamonte Structure

line 1 — the name of the first character
line 2 — two adjectives that describe that character
line 3 — three words that end in *ing* relating to that character
line 4 — four nouns, the first two relating to the character named in line 1 and the second two relating to the character named in line 7
line 5 — three words that end in *ing* relating to the second character
line 6 — two adjectives that describe the second character
line 7 — the name of the second character

Example: *Little House on the Prairie* by Laura Ingalls Wilder

Laura
Adventurous, mischievous
Exploring, fishing, playing
Friend, imp, helper, babysitter
Sewing, minding, studying
Gentle, dutiful
Mary

Write a diamonte comparing two characters from your book.

Title _____

Author _____

_____

_____

_____

_____

_____

_____

_____

Name _____

Beginning, Middle, and End

The **plot** tells what happens to the characters in a story. In most stories, the main character participates in a series of events including the buildup of a problem, the struggle to overcome it, and the resolution of the conflict.

Use pictures and words to tell about your book. You will need four sheets of plain white paper. Label three of the sheets **Beginning, Middle,** and **End**.

1. Make a title page out of the first sheet. Include the title of the book, author, your name, and the date. Illustrate this title page with a character or scene from the book.

2. At the top of the **Beginning** sheet, draw and color a picture showing an event from the beginning of the book. Beneath the picture, write a paragraph or two describing how the story began. Be sure to introduce your characters and describe the setting.

3. On the **Middle** sheet, draw and color a picture and write a paragraph or two describing the main event of the story.

4. On the **End** sheet, draw and color a picture and write a paragraph or two about how the story ends.

5. Staple the four sheets together.

6. Share your booklet with a friend.

Name _____

Sum It Up

Fill in the blanks with information about your book. Remember, the **main character** is the person, animal, or thing the story is about. A **minor character** interacts with the main character but is not the focus of the story. The **setting** is the location of the story. In the summary section on the next page, write briefly what the story is about, why you did or did not like the book, and any other points you think are important.

Title _____

Author _____

Main Character _____

_____

Minor Characters _____

_____

_____

Setting _____

_____

_____

Name _____

Sum It Up
(continued)

Summary _____

_____

_____

_____

_____

_____

_____

_____

_____

_____

_____

_____

_____

_____

Name _____

Short Takes

Write a two-sentence summary to capture the main idea of any three chapters in the book you just read.

Title _____

Author _____

Chapter Title or Number _____

Summary _____

_____

_____

_____

_____

Chapter Title or Number _____

Summary _____

_____

_____

_____

_____

Chapter Title or Number _____

Summary _____

_____

_____

_____

_____

_____

Name _____

Problems, Problems

Think about the most significant problem encountered by the main character in your book — what caused the problem, who was involved, and how it was solved.

Title _____

Author _____

1. Describe the problem. _____

   _____

   _____

   _____

2. How was the problem solved? _____

   _____

   _____

3. Describe a different solution to the problem. _____

   _____

   _____

4. How might your solution have changed the outcome of the book? _____

   _____

   _____

   _____

Name _____

Front Page Facts

On a large sheet of paper, design the front page of a newspaper based on the characters, events, and locations from your book.

Follow the sample on the next page to guide you in laying out your paper.

Title _____

Author _____

Include the following on your front page:

Flag: The flag is the name of a newspaper. Work your main character's name or hometown into the flag.
Example: *The Adventures of Tom Sawyer* – The St. Petersburg Sentinel

Banner Headline: This is a headline in large print briefly explaining what the lead story is about.

By-line: The name of the reporter is called his/her by-line.

Lead: A lead is the first sentence of a news story. The lead should include the answers to as many of the five W's (who, what, when, where, and why) as possible and an H (how).

Lead Story: The most important news of the day is called the lead story. It should tell about the main event in your book.

Cut: A picture or photograph related to the day's news is called a cut.

Cutline: The cutline is a sentence or two telling what is happening in the picture.

News Story: A news story is information about other interesting events of the day. Write at least two news stories based on events in your book.

Weather: The day's weather report gives information about conditions like snow, rain, sunshine, or storms.

St. Petersburg Sentinel

| Tuesday, July 21, 1875 | Circulation 52 | 2¢ a copy |

TOM AND HUCK FIND TREASURE!

by A. Reporter

Tom Sawyer and Huckleberry Finn show off the chest in which they found $12,000 in coins.

TREASURE FEVER BREAKS OUT!

by Ima Writer

Local citizens spurred by the news of robber's loot buried in MacDougal's Cave have begun to look for other troves.

Sheriff Hill cautioned searchers that vandals of vacant property may be prosecuted by the owners if trespassers are caught in the act.

"We ain't gonna let every fool who thinks he knows where there might be a treasure go diggin' up the town," Sheriff Hill said. "Folks may get hurt steppin' into all them holes and prowlin' around where they've no need to be."

Tom Sawyer and Huckleberry Finn discovered $12,000 in a buried treasure chest in MacDougal's Cave yesterday.

The coins, found in a soggy old chest, were thought to be loot hidden by the Murrel gang when they were operating in this area.

When questioned, Tom said that he discovered a clue leading to the treasure when he and Becky Thatcher were lost in the cave last week.

Tom and Huck entered the cave through the opening he and Becky used to escape. Using kite string to keep from losing their way, the boys found the treasure buried under the sign of the cross.

The box weighed 50 pounds, but the boys were able to put the coins in sacks they brought with them and carry them out of the cave.

Judge Thatcher stated that since the money cannot be traced to its original owners, the $12,000 will be split between Tom and Huck.

WEATHER

Granny Hunt's bunions have been acting up again—a sure sign of rain.

LONG-RANGE FORECAST—There are an unusually large number of nuts on the trees—a hard winter is coming!

JUDGE THATCHER PREDICTS ROSY FUTURE FOR TOM SAWYER

by Penn Mann

Judge Thatcher, who is personally supervising the investment of Tom Sawyer's money, said today that he believes the boy will "go far."

"Tom is a natural leader," the Judge said. "Why, just look at the way he got my daughter out of MacDougal's Cave. I would like to recommend him for the national military academy or encourage him to become a lawyer."

Name _____

Order, Please!

Chronological order is the sequence in which events happen. List eight of the most important incidents from your book in chronological order on the lines below. Then, on a separate piece of white art paper, illustrate these eight key events from your book.

Title _____

Author _____

1. _____

2. _____

3. _____

4. _____

5. _____

6. _____

7. _____

8. _____

Name _____

Five W's Poem

A **Five W's Poem** is a five-line poem that answers the questions Who? What?
When? Where? and Why? When finished, the poem should form one long sentence.
It does not have to rhyme.

STRUCTURE: line 1   **Who** or what is the poem about?
              line 2   **What** is he or she doing?
              line 3   **When** does the action take place?
              line 4   **Where** does it take place?
              line 5   **Why** does it take place?

Here is an example based on *The Sign of the Beaver* by Elizabeth
George Speare:

Who?	Twelve-year-old Matt
What?	is left to fend for himself
When?	for many months
Where?	in a lonely cabin in the Maine woods
Why?	waiting for Pa to return with the family

Write a Five W's Poem to summarize the plot of your book. (Leave out the "W"
word before each line.)

Title _____

Author _____

_____

_____

_____

_____

_____

Name _____

Conversation Piece

Draw two cartoons showing separate incidents from your book. Show the characters and the action. Write what is being said in bubbles.

Title _____

Author _____

1. Incident _____

   Characters involved _____

2. Incident _____

Characters involved _____

Name _____

Playing Favorites

Think about a favorite part of your book. Complete the following:

Title _____

Author _____

1. What characters were involved? _____
   _____

2. Describe the setting. _____
   _____
   _____

3. Describe exactly what happened. _____
   _____
   _____
   _____
   _____
   _____
   _____

4. How did you feel after you read this part? Why?_____
   _____
   _____
   _____

5. Why did you like this part of the book so much? _____
   _____
   _____
   _____
   _____

Name _____

Photo Essay

Choose four key events from your book. Draw one event in each of the photo borders below. Write a caption underneath each picture describing the event.

Title _____   Author _____

_____

_____

_____

_____

Name _____

From Start to Finish

The **setting** of a book is both the time and place of the action. The time can be a specific hour, day, date, or a general period in history or the future. The place can be a city, the countryside, a cave, or even outer space. The place can be real or fictional.

Describe the opening and closing settings in the book you have just read. Then, on a separate piece of white art paper, illustrate these two settings.

Title _____

Author _____

Opening Setting

Time _____

_____

Place _____

_____

Closing Setting

Time _____

_____

Place _____

_____

Name _____

On Location

Choose one of your favorite settings from the book you read. Find four descriptive passages that helped you see the scene in your mind. On the lines provided, copy each passage and its page reference.

> Here are two examples from *The Sign of the Beaver* by Elizabeth George Speare:
>
> page 1   ...behind the cabin were the mounds of corn...and the pumpkin vines just showing between the stumps of trees.
>
> page 3   ...it had only one room...inside there were shelves along one wall and a sturdy puncheon table with two stools...against the wall was a chimney of smaller logs, daubed and lined with clay from the creek.

Title _____

Author _____

Setting _____

_____

1. page ____ _____

_____

2. page ____ _____

_____

3. page ____ _____

_____

4. page ____ _____

_____

Name _____

Change of Place

Think of an event in your book in which the setting directly affected the outcome of the story. What if the incident had happened in a different place? Would the characters have acted differently? Would the incident have turned out the same way?

Briefly describe the event as it actually happened. Then choose a new setting for the event, describe it, and write a new outcome.

Title _____

Author _____

Event _____

Original Setting: _____

_____

Original Outcome: _____

_____

_____

_____

_____

New Setting: _____

_____

New Outcome: _____

_____

_____

_____

_____

Name _____

Time Flies

Choose your favorite character from your book and show how the author describes the passing of time in that character's life. List in chronological order six important things your character did that refer to the time of day, a season, or a particular year.

Title _____

Author _____

Character _____

Character's actions in chronological order:

1. _____
   _____
2. _____
   _____
3. _____
   _____
4. _____
   _____
5. _____
   _____
6. _____
   _____

1945 AIR RACE

Name _____

Classified Ads

Pretend you work for a real estate agency. You have been asked to write classified ads to sell two different properties from your book. Make each ad as descriptive as possible using 30 words or less.

> **Example:**
>
> Property: Grandfather's farm from *Stone Fox by* John
>   Reynolds Gardiner
>
> **FOR SALE:** Small potato farm; Teton Mountains of Wyoming; two-bedroom frame house with a stone chimney; underground shed; chicken coop and garden; lovely secluded location.

Title _____

Author _____

AD #1
Property: _____

For Sale: _____

_____

_____

_____

_____

AD #2
Property: _____

For Sale: _____

_____

_____

_____

_____

Name _____

Blast from the Past

Read a book that was written more than twenty-five years ago. Answer the questions below.

Title _____

Author _____ Date published _____

1. Why do you think this book continues to be popular after such a long time?

   _____

   _____

   _____

2. Could the main events in the book have happened in another time? _____

   Why or why not? _____

   _____

3. Find three things in the book that show it was not written recently. Watch for references to clothing styles, vehicles, prices, products, or hairstyles as well as slang terms or patterns of speech that might date your book. You may use both the text and illustrations as examples. Write the three things you find and give a page reference for each example.

   page _____ _____

   page _____ _____

   page _____ _____

4. If this book were rewritten today, describe three things that might be changed or added to update the story.

   _____

   _____

   _____

Name _____

Where It Happened

Choose two different settings from your book. Identify each setting, write a one-sentence description of it, and describe the major events that took place there.

Title _____

Author _____

Setting #1 _____

   Description _____

_____

   Events _____

_____

_____

_____

_____

_____

Setting #2 _____

   Description _____

_____

   Events _____

_____

_____

_____

_____

_____

Name _____

Take a Trip

Imagine that you are a character from your book. Design a picture postcard to send to another character in the book. Draw and color a picture showing the setting of one of the major events in the story on the front of the card shown below. On the next page, write a message and address the card to the character you have chosen. Design a postage stamp for your postcard.

Title _____

Author _____

Name _____

Take a Trip
(continued)

Name _____

The Way It Might Have Been

Sometimes the time that an incident takes place has an effect on the outcome of the action. Think of an important event in your book. Imagine that the event had taken place at a different time. How might this change in time affect the outcome of the story?

Title _____

Author _____

Event _____

_____

_____

The Way It Was

1. Time _____

_____

_____

2. Outcome _____

_____

_____

_____

_____

_____

Name _____

The Way It Might Have Been
(continued)

The Way It Might Have Been

1. New Time _____

_____

_____

2. New Outcome _____

_____

_____

_____

_____

_____

_____

_____

Name _____

List...List...List

Look through your book to find and list five words that fit in each of the categories below. On a separate piece of paper, use these words to create a word search puzzle for a friend.

Title _____

Author _____

Living Things

_____

_____

_____

_____

_____

Settings

_____

_____

_____

_____

_____

Careers

_____

_____

_____

_____

_____

Foods

_____

_____

_____

_____

_____

Name _____

Don't Say That!

There are many ways to indicate that a character has spoken besides using the word *said*. Look through your book to find four examples of words other than *said* that show a character is speaking. Write the quotation and the page on which it appears.

Title _____

Author _____

> **Example:** *Banner in the Sky* by James Ramsey Ullman
>
> page 29 - the voice *answered*   page 41 - he *demanded*
> page 37 - he *murmured*   page 101 - Saxo *grunted*

Page Number   Quotation

_____   _____

_____   _____

_____   _____

_____   _____

Find four quotations from your book in which the author uses the word *said* to show who is speaking. Replace each *said* with a more unique word, give the page reference, and write the new quotation.

> **Example:** *Banner in the Sky*
>
> page 29 - Original quotation: "No, it is not so steep," *said* Rudy.
>   New quotation: "No, it is not so steep," *agreed* Rudy.

Page Number   New Quotation

_____   _____

_____   _____

_____   _____

_____   _____

Name _____

Word Search

Look through your book and find three words that fit each of the following categories. Write the words you find in the boxes below.

Title _____

Author _____

three-syllable words	
Word	Page
_____	_____
_____	_____
_____	_____

compound words	
Word	Page
_____	_____
_____	_____
_____	_____

proper nouns	
Word	Page
_____	_____
_____	_____

ten-letter words	
Word	Page
_____	_____
_____	_____

Name _____

Word Search
(continued)

words that start and end with the same letter	
Word	Page
_____	_____
_____	_____
_____	_____

words that have more than one meaning	
Word	Page
_____	_____
_____	_____
_____	_____

words that can make an anagram*		
Word	Anagram	Page
_____	_____	_____
_____	_____	_____
_____	_____	_____

* An **anagram** is a word that is made by rearranging and using all of the letters of another word (example: steam - meats).

Name _____

In Other Words

Writers like to make their stories as colorful and descriptive as possible. One tool that helps them accomplish this is a thesaurus. A **thesaurus** is a book that lists words alphabetically and provides synonyms for them. Using a thesaurus, you can replace words with more interesting synonyms. For example, the *three little pigs* might become a *trio of petite porkers.*

Choose a paragraph from your book. Use a thesaurus to help you rewrite the paragraph by substituting synonyms for as many words as possible.

Title _____

Author _____

Page number _____

_____

_____

_____

_____

_____

_____

_____

_____

_____

_____

_____

Name _____

Style Show

Read two books by the same author. Compare the books by answering the questions below. Think about characters, setting, plot, and the author's style of writing.

Title _____

Title _____

Author _____

1. How were the books alike? _____

   _____

   _____

   _____

   _____

2. How were the books different? _____

   _____

   _____

   _____

   _____

3. Which book did you like better? _____

   _____

   Why? _____

   _____

   _____

   _____

Name _____

Cover Story

Design a new cover for the book you have just read. Be sure to include the title, the author's name, and an illustration. Use the characters, an event, or a setting from your book in your cover design. Then, on a separate sheet of paper, write a "blurb" about the book for the inside panel that will make others want to read your book .

Name _____

Design a Display

The author's hometown library has decided to set up a display for each of his/her books. Each display will feature four items that have special meaning in the book. You have been asked to make a display for the book you have read. List the items you would choose and explain why you selected them for the display.

Title _____

Author _____

1. Item _____

   Reason _____

   _____

2. Item _____

   Reason _____

   _____

3. Item _____

   Reason _____

   _____

4. Item _____

   Reason _____

   _____

Name _____

Best-Seller T-Shirt

The book you have read has been such a success that the publisher has decided to sell a series of products based on the book and its characters. One item that is sure to be a hit is the *Best-Seller T-Shirt*. Design a T-shirt that shows an event, the setting, or a character from the book.

Name _____

Second Edition

The publisher has decided to print a longer version of the book you have just read. You have been asked to come up with ideas for two additional chapters. These two chapters may be added at any point in the story (before the original story begins, in the middle, or after the story ends). Write a short summary of your idea for each chapter. Tell where the new chapters would fit best in the book.

Title _____

Author _____

Chapter A _____

_____

_____

_____

_____

_____

_____

Chapter B _____

_____

_____

_____

_____

_____

_____

Name _____

Reader's Review

Pretend you are the book reviewer for a school newspaper. Write a short summary that will make students want to read your book. Design your own rating system that uses pictures or symbols to show how you felt about the book.

Title _____

Author _____

_____

_____

_____

_____

_____

_____

_____

_____

_____

_____

_____

_____

_____

_____

_____

_____

Name _____

Ten Questions

Pretend you have been asked to write questions based on your book for a popular television quiz show. Each question should have a one-word answer. Make a numbered answer key on the back of this page. Test your questions on a classmate who has read the same book.

Title _____

Author _____

1. _____
2. _____
3. _____
4. _____
5. _____
6. _____
7. _____
8. _____
9. _____
10. _____

Newbery Medal Winners

Year	Title	Author
1922	The Story of Mankind	Hendrik van Loon
1923	The Voyages of Dr. Doolittle	Hugh Lofting
1924	The Dark Frigate	Charles Hawes
1925	Tales from Silver Lands	Charles Finger
1926	Shen of the Sea	Arthur Chrisman
1927	Smoky	Will James
1928	Gay-Neck, The Story of a Pigeon	Dhan Gopal Mukerji
1929	The Trumpeter of Krakow	Eric P. Kelly
1930	Hitty, Her First Hundred Years	Rachel Field
1931	The Cat Who Went to Heaven	Elizabeth Coatsworth
1932	Waterless Mountain	Laura Adams Armer
1933	Young Fu of the Upper Yangtze	Elizabeth Lewis
1934	Invincible Louisa	Cornelia Meigs
1935	Dobry	Monica Shannon
1936	Caddie Woodlawn	Carol Ryrie Brink
1937	Roller Skates	Ruth Sawyer
1938	The White Stag	Kate Seredy
1939	Thimble Summer	Elizabeth Enright
1940	Daniel Boone	James Daugherty
1941	Call it Courage	Armstrong Sperry
1942	The Matchlock Gun	Walter D. Edmonds
1943	Adam of the Road	Elizabeth Janet Gray
1944	Johnny Tremain	Esther Forbes
1945	Rabbit Hill	Robert Lawson
1946	Strawberry Girl	Lois Lenski
1947	Miss Hickory	Carolyn Sherwin Bailey
1948	The Twenty-One Balloons	William Péne du Bois
1949	King of the Wind	Marguerite Henry
1950	The Door in the Wall	Marguerite de Angeli
1951	Amos Fortune, Free Man	Elizabeth Yates
1952	Ginger Pye	Eleanor Estes
1953	Secret of the Andes	Ann Nolan Clark
1954	...And Now Miguel	Joseph Krumgold
1955	The Wheel on the School	Meindert DeJong
1956	Carry On, Mr. Bowditch	Jean Lee Latham
1957	Miracles on Maple Hill	Virginia Sorensen
1958	Rifles for Watie	Harold V. Keith
1959	The Witch of Blackbird Pond	Elizabeth George Speare
1960	Onion John	Joseph Krumgold
1961	Island of the Blue Dolphins	Scott O'Dell
1962	The Bronze Bow	Elizabeth George Speare
1963	A Wrinkle in Time	Madeleine L'Engle
1964	It's Like This, Cat	Emily C. Neville
1965	Shadow of a Bull	Maia Wojciechowska
1966	I, Juan de Pareja	Elizabeth Borton de Treviño
1967	Up a Road Slowly	Irene Hunt

Name _____

Newbery Medal Winners

Year	Title	Author
1968	From the Mixed-Up Files of Mrs. Basil E. Frankweiler	Elaine Konigsburg
1969	The High King	Lloyd Alexander
1970	Sounder	William H. Armstrong
1971	The Summer of the Swans	Betsy Byars
1972	Mrs. Frisby and the Rats of NIMH	Robert C. O'Brien
1973	Julie of the Wolves	Jean Craighead George
1974	The Slave Dancer	Paula Fox
1975	M.C. Higgins, the Great	Virginia Hamilton
1976	The Grey King	Susan Cooper
1977	Roll of Thunder, Hear My Cry	Mildred D. Taylor
1978	Bridge to Terabithia	Katherine Paterson
1979	The Westing Game	Ellen Raskin
1980	A Gathering of Days: A New England Girl's Journal	Joan Blos
1981	Jacob Have I Loved	Katherine Paterson
1982	A Visit to William Blake's Inn	Nancy Willard
1983	Dicey's Song	Cynthia Voigt
1984	Dear Mr. Henshaw	Beverly Cleary
1985	The Hero and the Crown	Robin McKinley
1986	Sarah, Plain and Tall	Patricia MacLachlan
1987	The Whipping Boy	Sid Fleischman
1988	Lincoln: A Photobiography	Russell Freedman
1989	Joyful Noise: Poems for Two Voices	Paul Fleischman
1990	Number the Stars	Lois Lowry
1991	Maniac C. Magee	Jerry Spinelli
1992	Shiloh	Phyllis R. Naylor
1993	Missing May	Cynthia Rylant

Newbery Honor Books

Year	Title	Author
1960	My Side of the Mountain	Jean George
	America is Born	Gerald W. Johnson
	The Gammage Cup	Carol Kendall
1961	America Moves Forward	Gerald W. Johnson
	Cricket in Times Square	George Selden
	Old Ramon	Jack Schaefer
1962	Frontier Living	Edwin Tunis
	The Golden Goblet	Eloise Jarvis McGraw
	Belling the Tiger	Mary Stolz
1963	Thistle and Thyme	Leclaire Alger
	Men of Athens	Olivia Coolidge
1964	Rascal	Sterling North
	The Loner	Ester Wier
1965	Across Five Aprils	Irene Hunt

Newbery Honor Books

Year	Title	Author
1966	The Animal Farm	Randall Jarrell
	The Black Cauldron	Lloyd Alexander
	The Noonday Friends	Mary Stolz
1967	The Jazz Man	Mary Hays Weik
	Zlateh the Goat	Isaac B. Singer
1968	Jennifer, Hecate, Macbeth, William McKinley, and Me, Elizabeth	Elaine Konigsburg
1969	To Be a Slave	Julius Lester
	When Schlemiel Went to Warsaw	Isaac B. Singer
1970	Journey Outside	Mary Q. Steele
	Our Eddie	Sulamith Ish-Kishor
	The Many Ways of Seeing	Janet Gaylord Moore
1971	Enchantress from the Stars	Sylvia L. Engdahl
	Kneeknock Rise	Natalie Babbitt
	Sing Down the Moon	Scott O'Dell
1972	Annie and the Old One	Miska Miles
	Incident at Hawk's Hill	Allan W. Eckert
	The Headless Cupid	Zilpha Snyder
	The Planet of Junior Brown	Virginia Hamilton
1973	Frog and Toad Together	Arnold Lobel
	The Upstairs Room	Johanna Reiss
	The Witches of Worm	Zilpha Snyder
1974	The Dark is Rising	Susan Cooper
1975	Figgs & Phantoms	Ellen Raskin
	My Brother Sam is Dead	James & Christopher Collier
	Phillip Hall Likes Me, I Reckon Maybe	Bette Greene
	The Perilous Gard	Elizabeth M. Pope
1976	The Hundred Penny Box	Sharon B. Mathis
	Dragonwings	Laurence Yep
1977	A String in the Harp	Nancy Bond
	Abel's Island	William Steig
1978	Ramona and Her Father	Beverly Cleary
	Anpao: An American Indian Odyssey	Jamake Highwater
1979	The Great Gilly Hopkins	Katherine Paterson
1980	The Road from Home	David Kherdian
1981	The Fledgling	Jane Langton
	A Ring of Endless Light	Madeleine L'Engle
1982	Ramona Quimby, Age 8	Beverly Cleary
	Upon the Head of the Goat	Aranka Siegal
1983	Graven Images	Paul Fleischman
	Homesick, My Own Story	Jean Fritz
	Sweet Whisper, Brother Rush	Virginia Hamilton
	The Blue Sword	Robin McKinley
	Doctor DeSoto	William Steig

Name _____

Newbery Honor Books

Year	Title	Author
1984	The Wish Giver	Bill Brittain
	Sugaring Time	Kathryn Lasky
	The Sign of the Beaver	Elizabeth George Speare
	A Solitary Blue	Cynthia Voigt
1985	The Moves Make the Man	Bruce Brooks
	One-Eyed Cat	Paula Fox
	Like Jake and Me	Mavis Jukes
1986	Commodore Perry in the Land of the Shogun	Rhoda Blumberg
	Dogsong	Gary Paulsen
1987	A Fine White Dust	Cynthia Rylant
	Volcano	Patricia Lauber
	On My Honor	Marion Dane Bauer
1988	After the Rain	Norma Fox Mazer
	Hatchet	Gary Paulsen
1989	In the Beginning: Creation Stories from Around the World	Virginia Hamilton
	Scorpions	Walter Dean Myers
1990	Afternoon of the Elves	Janet Taylor Lisle
	Shabanu: Daughter of the Wind	Suzanne F. Staples
	The Winter Room	Gary Paulsen
1991	The True Confessions of Charlotte Doyle	Avi
1992	Nothing But the Truth	Avi
	Wright Brothers: How They Invented the Airplane	Russell Freedman
1993	The Dark Thirty	Patricia McKissack
	Somewhere in the Darkness	Walter Dean Myers
	What Hearts	Bruce Brooks

More Great Reading!

Title	Author
Aesop's Fables	Fritz Kredel
Alice in Wonderland	Lewis Carroll
All Things Bright and Beautiful	James Herriot
Amy's Eyes	Richard Kennedy
Anne Frank, The Diary of a Young Girl	Anne Frank
Anne of Green Gables	L.M. Montgomery
Are You There God? It's Me, Margaret	Judy Blume
Arthur, for the Very First Time	Patricia MacLachlan
Beezus and Ramona	Beverly Cleary
The Black Stallion	Walter Farley
The Book of Three (Prydain Chronicles)	Lloyd Alexander
Boy's King Arthur	Sir Thomas Malory

Name _____

More Great Reading!

Title	Author
The Cabin Faced West	Jean Fritz
The Cat Ate My Gymsuit	Paul Danziger
The Cay	Theodore Taylor
Charlotte's Web	E.B. White
Circle of Fire	William H. Hooks
Clan of the Cave Bear	Jean Auel
Daniel Boone	James Daugherty
The Enormous Egg	Oliver Butterworth
Freaky Friday	Mary Rodgers
Hazel Rye	Vera & Bill Cleaver
Henry Huggins	Beverly Cleary
The Hobbit	J.R.R. Tolkien
How to Eat Fried Worms	Thomas Rockwell
The Indian in the Cupboard	Lynne Reid Banks
Ishi: Last of the Tribe	Theodore Kroeber
James and the Giant Peach	Roald Dahl
The Jungle Book	Rudyard Kipling
Kon-Tiki	Thor Heyerdahl
Lassie Come Home	Eric M. Knight
The Legend of Sleepy Hollow	Washington Irving
The Lion, the Witch, and the Wardrobe	C.S. Lewis
Little House on the Prairie (series)	Laura Ingalls Wilder
Little Women	Louisa May Alcott
My Friend Flicka	Mary Sture-Vasa
Nobody's Family is Going to Change	Louise Fitzhugh
Nothing's Fair in Fifth Grade	Barte DeClements
Old Yeller	Fred Gipson
The Outsiders	S.E. Hinton
Paddle to the Sea	Holling Clancy Holling
Rabbit Hill	Robert Lawson
Ramona and Her Mother	Beverly Cleary
Rebecca of Sunnybrook Farm	Kate Wiggins
Robin Hood: His Life and Legend	Bernard Miles
Sarah Crewe	Frances Hodgson Burnett
The Secret Garden	Frances Hodgson Burnett
Stone Fox	John Reynolds Gardiner
Stuart Little	E.B. White
Superfudge	Judy Blume
Tales of a Fourth Grade Nothing	Judy Blume
Thirteen Ways to Sink a Sub	Jamie Gilson
Trouble River	Betsy Byars
Trumpet of the Swan	E.B. White
Tuck Everlasting	Natalie Babbitt
Where the Red Fern Grows	Wilson Rawls
Wind in the Willows	Kenneth Grahame
The Wizard of Oz	L. Frank Baum

Student Record Sheet for _____

(name of student)

Book Title	Author	Page Number	Character-ization	Plot	Setting	Just For Fun	Grade	Date

READING CERTIFICATE

This certifies that_____has read ____books.

Reading Award

presented to _____ for reading _____ books.

Bookworks
© 1993—The Learning Works, Inc.